Hi! My name is Pontus, what's yours?

Free Support Videos at
www.MusicolorMethod.com

PIANO FOR KIDS

Teach Complete Beginners How To Play Instantly With The Musicolor Method®

FOR PRESCHOOLERS, GRADE SCHOOLERS & BEYOND

By Andrew Ingkavet

MUSICOLOR METHOD PIANO SONGBOOK - VOLUME 1

* Not for penguins

HOW THIS BOOK IS ORGANIZED

This book has 3 sections:

❋ Introductory Materials & Setup

❋ Student Songs & Activities with Lesson Notes

❋ Parent/Teacher Appendix

WHAT YOU NEED

- A piano or digital keyboard

- Color coding stickers
  or masking tape with crayons

- Washable scented markers for painting fingernails

OPTIONAL

- Colored pencils for coloring

- Stickers for rewards

How The Musicolor Method Works

Color on Hands	Color on Keys	Color on Pages

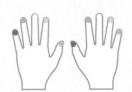

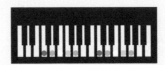

Published by Musicolor Method, a division of 300 Monks, LLC. 114 Garfield Place, 3R,
Brooklyn, NY 11215, USA | Email: hello@musicolormethod.com

Visit our website: www.musicolormethod.com for free videos to help
Musicolor Method® is a registered trademark of 300 Monks, LLC

TABLE OF CONTENTS

Introductory Materials & Setup

Title Page + Name Slot --1

How This Book Is Organized --2

What You Need --2

Copyright ---2

Table of Contents --3

Dedication & Acknowledgements --4

Introduction---5

What Makes This Unique? --6

Is Your Child Ready? --6

Why The Musicolor Method® Works --7

Why Every Child Should Begin With Piano --8

Setting Up Keys & Fingers ---9

Trace Hands --10

Student Songs & Activities

☐ Song 1 - What's Your Favorite Ice Cream? --13

☐ Song 2 - Birthday Cake--15

☐ Song 3 - Let's Jump In The Pool and Play ---17

☐ Song 4 - Dinah ---19

☐ Song 5 - Who's That Tapping? ---21

☐ Song 6 - Orange Who? --23

☐ Song 7 - Red Is For Apples --25

☐ Song 8 - Ants In My Pants ---27

☐ Song 9 - Bingo Bongo Boom --29

☐ Song 10 - The Zebra Who Only Ate Pizza ---31

☐ Achievement Certificate ---35

Parent / Teacher Appendix

Songs in Standard Notation --37

Practice Tips--40

Practice Chart ---42

DEDICATION

To my friend, guide, mentor, high school music teacher, the late great Andy Blackett...thank you.

ACKNOWLEDGEMENTS

Thank you to the parents of all the students I have worked with over the years. Thank you to all the music teachers around the world who are using the Musicolor Method® to bring joy and life skills to so many. Thank you to all my students!

Thank you to my father and mother for giving me the seeds of music and encouraging my passions.

Thank you to Alejandro and Monica, I love you both so much.

Thank you to my branding guru/designer and brother, Steve Ingkavet!

Thank you to my book launch team: Anne Vardanega, Marcie Estes, Nicole Clark, Melonie Collmann, Sudiksha Joshi, Ali Watts Sise.

Thank you Brett Crudgington, Susan Petters, Carol Koczo, Esther Farkas, Igor Mitrovic, Adam Holmes, Susan Soltano, Erin Soltano for proofreading, design comments and beta testing.

Cover and Logo design: Steve Ingkavet

Book Design, Layout & Illustrations: Andrew Ingkavet

Additional Illustrations by Steve Ingkavet

Back Cover Photo: Michelle Ingkavet Cavanagh

INTRODUCTION

My son Alejandro entered the world singing. Ever since I can remember, we sang to him, and he sang back. When he turned three, he began asking for music lessons. Even though I had trained to be a music teacher at NYU (Scholar in Education), I had never made that my professional focus. I figured I'd just get him a local teacher. To my surprise, not a single teacher would accept a three year old. They would say, "Come back when he's eight."

So I decided to make teaching my son a home-school project. I pulled out all my old music education textbooks, dove deep into the library, and spent thousands of hours (and dollars!) researching methods, materials, and curriculum.

What I discovered was... a gap in music education.

There were plenty of toddler clap-along and sing-along programs, but no one presented a viable curriculum to teach a preschooler how to play an instrument. The more I experimented, though, the more I knew it was possible.

Today, I've spent over a decade with music education as my primary professional focus. I've gone from a handful of children to a thriving music school with several teachers and close to 100 students per week. The Musicolor Method® is now being taught worldwide with incredible results.

By following along with simple proven songs and activities in sequence, I am confident that you can successfully introduce the magic of music to your child / student.

And my son? I'm happy and proud to say he is growing up into a fine young man and accomplished musician who still sings everyday!

I wish you the best with your musical magical journey!

Best,

Andrew Ingkavet
Brooklyn, NY
May 2018

WHAT MAKES THIS UNIQUE?

Does your child show an interest in music but you're not quite sure about diving into music lessons? Or have you already tried teaching them yourself only to end up in frustration or worse...tears?

This book and the Musicolor Method® can help!

We start with playing first.

We use color on keys, fingers, and a simple notation. Color is direct labelling and creates a scaffolding for children to quickly figure out what to do. It makes learning to play fast, fun, and intuitive.

Using the simple proven approach in this book, you can teach your preschool child (and yourself), to play piano (or keyboard) while beginning to learn about the fundamentals of music.

Each song is a finger exercise in disguise. You should only work on one per week. This allows your child to build up the strength and dexterity to tackle a new pattern the following week. Try not to speed through.

IS YOUR CHILD READY?

This method works for kids 4 years old and up. Sometimes, even 3 year olds.

Check to see if your child...

Recognizes basic colors and their names: red, orange, yellow, green, blue, purple

Recognizes and can name the letters of the alphabet, at least from A to G

Knows the sequence of the alphabet A to G

Can pick up small objects with their fingers and/or write their name

Can count to 10

Can focus on one activity for 5 minutes

If they can do the above, then this method can be used with almost any child. I've also had great success with special needs children on the autism spectrum.

Even if you have had little or no musical training, you can teach yourself the basics.

Because the graphics are so simple, young children "read the music" even if they can't read words.

They instantly know what to play and practice without help from an adult.

WHY THE  MUSICOLOR METHOD WORKS

We created a visual way to communicate sound with color.

Kids make direct connections from sheet music to keys to fingers.

We bypass symbols like letter names, clef signs and staff and get right to playing music. The direct labeling and color scaffolding make learning fun, fast and easy.

Even preliterate and special-needs students can use this. They intuitively understand and know what to play. This gives instant confidence.

They can practice on their own!

Progress is rapid. By playing simple songs over and over, students can memorize a repertoire of songs and begin honing technique.

Each lesson adds new patterns. Eventually, we add details like structure, rhythm, harmony and more.

There are six phases of Musicolor Notation™. This book covers phase one.

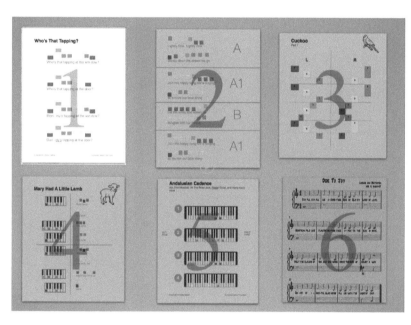

How The Musicolor Method Works

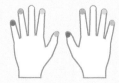

WHY EVERY CHILD SHOULD BEGIN WITH PIANO

We recommend every child to start learning music with a piano (or keyboard).

There are many reasons:

1. The keyboard is visual and logically organized making comprehension much easier.

2. It doesn't require a lot of physical effort to produce a pleasing sound.

3. Concepts of music theory, especially intervals, harmony and chords, can be explained spatially and visually. These concepts can then be transferred to other instruments.

4. Every note in the orchestra can be produced on the piano. It's why composers use the piano and every music major studies piano.

SETTING UP KEYS & FINGERS

ORDER OF COLORS

We use five colors to match the five fingers of each hand.

1. Red (C)

2. Orange (D)

3. Yellow (E)

4. Green (F)

5. Blue (G)

It's a rainbow!

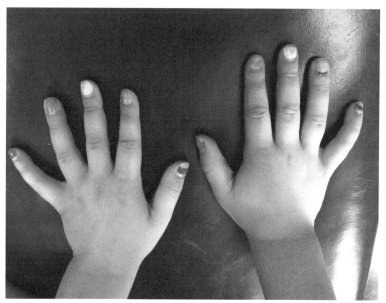

USE WASHABLE MARKERS OR CHILD-SAFE NAIL POLISH TO LABEL FINGERNAILS.
(OR EVEN STICKERS.)

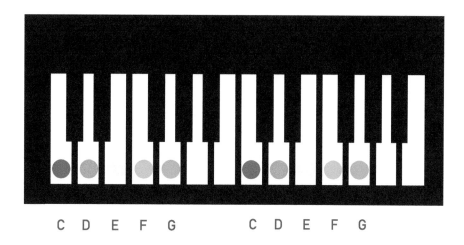

C D E F G   C D E F G

PLACE COLORS ON THE KEYS AS ABOVE

Trace Your Piano Hands!

Name

Date:

LEFT HAND

RIGHT HAND

※ *PAINT CHILD'S FINGERNAILS WITH WASHABLE MARKERS*
※ *TRACE THEIR HANDS HERE*
※ *COLOR FINGERS TO MATCH FINGERNAILS*
※ *MARK DATE*
※ *TELL THEM "ONE DAY YOU WILL BE AMAZED AT THE SIZE OF YOUR HANDS!"*

STUDENT SONGS & ACTIVITIES

1.Introduce

- Ask your child what their favorite ice cream flavor is.

- Tell them this song is about ice cream

2. Notice & Note

- Read and sing the words while pointing at each color box

- Alternatively, use the color names instead of lyrics

3. Demonstrate

- This first song introduces using all 10 fingers right away.

- Sing and play to demonstrate.

- Bounce the entire arm from the wrist.

- The objective is to have your child build up finger dexterity and the use of each finger for a specific key and color. This is called a 5 finger position and is based around middle C.

4. Now It's Your Turn

- Encourage them to sing and play at the same time. This keeps good rhythm.

- Gently correct the fingering - try to use the right color for the right finger.

5. Practice Notes

- Work on this one hand at a time. When it gets easy, try two hands together. Then, try it with eyes closed.

- After this becomes easy, start working on gently curving the fingers as if they were gently holding a ball of cotton candy.

- This song should be practiced everyday for at least the first week. Don't skip ahead. This is like taking your fingers to the piano gym.

- Then have them do it one hand at a time. After a few days/weeks, you can have them sing and play with both hands together.

- Coloring activity: ice cream cone.

What's Your Favorite Ice Cream?

What's your fav- -'rite ice cream?

What's your fav- -'rite ice cream?

What's your fav- -'rite ice cream?

What's your fav- -'rite ice cream?

What's your fav- -'rite ice cream?

Let's go eat some now!

1.Introduce

- Ask your child, "What is this a picture of?"

2. Notice & Note

- There are only three colors/notes in this song.

- Note: you may recognize this as a variation on Hot Cross Buns.

- See if your child can figure out what fingers to use on each hand.

- Then, read/sing each word while pointing to the color box.

3. Demonstrate

- Sing and play to demonstrate, then have them do it one hand at a time. After a few days/ weeks, you can have them sing and play with both hands together.

4. Now It's Your Turn

- Encourage them to sing and play at the same time. This keeps good rhythm.

- Gently correct the fingering - try to use the right color for the right finger.

5. Practice Notes

- Work on this one hand at a time. When it gets easy, try two hands together. Then, try it with eyes closed.

- After this becomes easy, start working on gently curving the fingers as if they were gently holding a ball of cotton candy.

- This song should be practiced everyday for at least the first week. Don't skip ahead. This is like taking your fingers to the piano gym.

- Then have them do it one hand at a time. After a few days/weeks, you can have them sing and play with both hands together.

- Coloring activity: birthday cake.

Birthday Cake

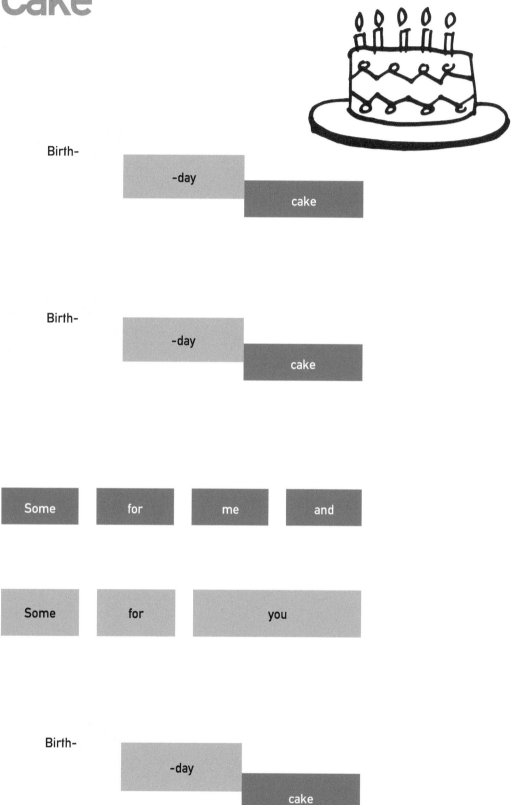

Birth- -day cake

Birth- -day cake

Some for me and

Some for you

Birth- -day cake

1.Introduce

- This song is about...swimming!

- Ask your child if they notice a pattern to the colors - it's like steps going up.

2. Notice & Note

- A new finger pattern that walks up and down the 5 finger C scale.

- Read/sing each word while pointing to the color box.

3. Demonstrate

- Sing and play to demonstrate, then have them do it one hand at a time. After a few days/ weeks, you can have them sing and play with both hands together.

- The object here is to drop your arms on the first note and roll up (or down) to the next notes.

- Watch the accompanying video for more detail.

4. Now It's Your Turn

- Encourage them to sing and play at the same time. This keeps good rhythm.

- Gently correct the fingering - try to use the right color for the right finger.

5. Practice Notes

- Work on this one hand at a time. When it gets easy, try two hands together. Then, try it with eyes closed.

- Coloring activity: Sun, Pontus in the pool.

Let's Jump In The Pool and Play

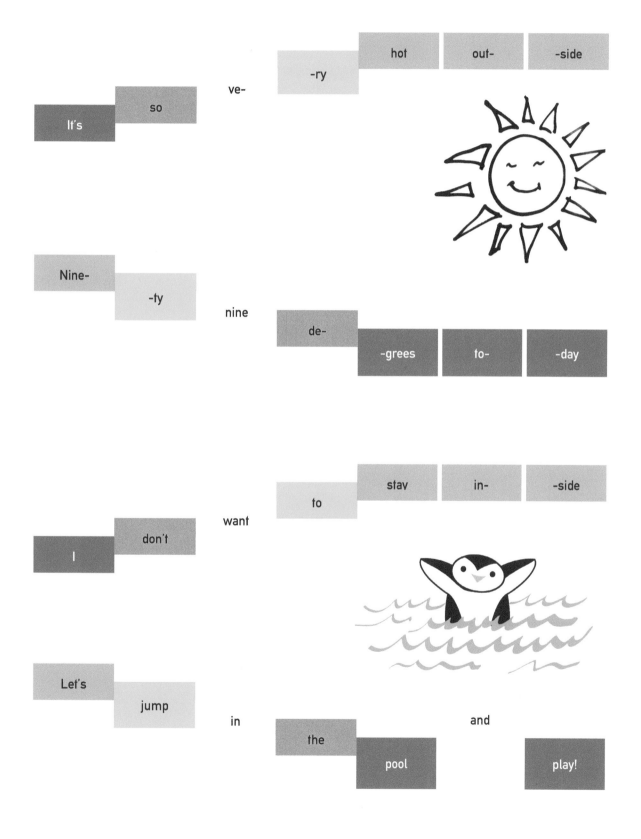

ve- -ry hot out- -side

It's so

Nine- -ty nine de- -grees to- -day

to stay in- -side

I don't want

Let's jump in the pool and play!

1.Introduce

- Does your child know what a banjo is?

- Try searching for banjo images and videos online.

- Ask your child if they notice a pattern to the colors.

2. Notice & Note

- Point to the first line and ask your child "How many red boxes are on this first line?"

- Do you notice something about the other lines? They also have five red boxes.

- But notice the last line is very different.

- Ask your child, have you ever seen the pattern at the end of the song? (Birthday Cake)

3. Demonstrate

- Sing and play to demonstrate.

- A bouncy pattern followed by skipping keys/notes.

- Bounce your arms for the repeated red notes.

4. Now It's Your Turn

- Encourage them to sing and play at the same time. This keeps good rhythm.

- Gently correct the fingering - try to use the right color for the right finger.

5. Practice Notes

- Work on this one hand at a time. When it gets easy, try two hands together. Then, try it with eyes closed.

- Coloring activity: Banjo.

Dinah

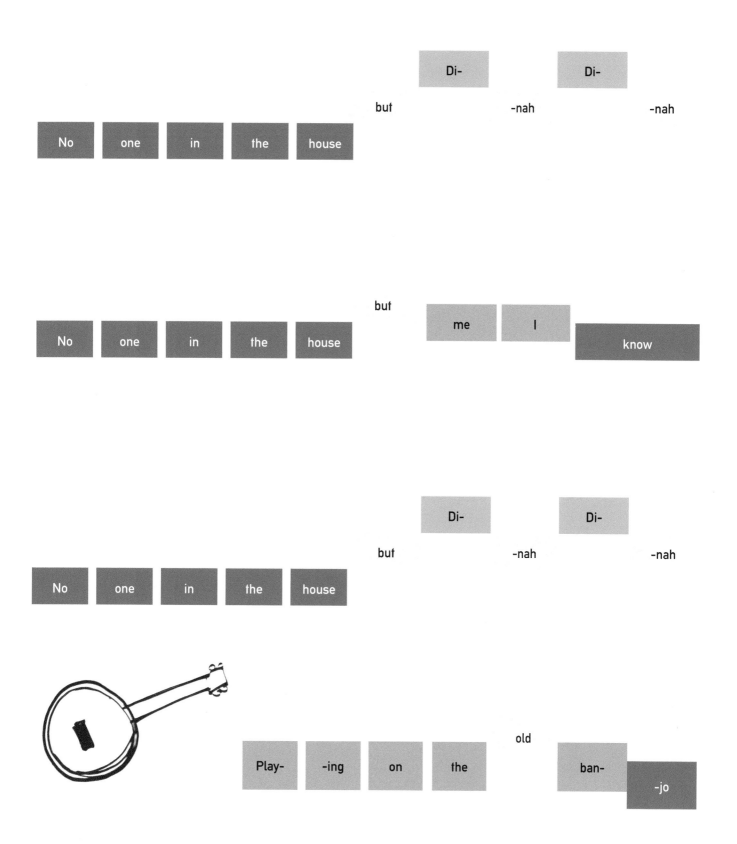

1.Introduce

- This song is a story about someone knocking at the door and the window.

- Ask, "What happens if I forget my keys?"

2. Notice & Note

- Point out that this song has a lot of similar patterns.

- Notice how every line starts with red, then goes to blue, etc.

- The only difference is the end of each line.

- By having them notice the patterns, they begin to understand the structure of songs. This aids in memorization and ability to retain longer phrases in memory.

3. Demonstrate

- Read/sing the words to them while pointing to each box.

- Sing and play to demonstrate.

4. Now It's Your Turn

- Encourage them to sing and play at the same time. This keeps good rhythm.

- Gently correct the fingering - try to use the right color for the right finger.

5. Practice Notes

- Work on this one hand at a time. When it gets easy, try two hands together. Then, try it with eyes closed.

- Coloring activity: Pontus in the window.

Who's That Tapping?

Who's that tap- -ping at the win- -dow?

Who's that tap- -ping at the door?

Mom- -my's tap- -ping at the win- -dow

Dad- -dy's tap- -ping at the door

1.Introduce

- This song is based on the old children's knock-knock jokes.

- Note the joke is that "orange"sounds similar to "aren't you?"

2. Notice & Note

- Ask your child if they notice a pattern.

- Read/sing the words to them while pointing to each box.

3. Demonstrate

- Read/sing the words to them while pointing to each box.

- Sing and play to demonstrate.

4. Now It's Your Turn

- Encourage them to sing and play at the same time. This keeps good rhythm.

- Gently correct the fingering - try to use the right color for the right finger.

5. Practice Notes

- Work on this one hand at a time. When it gets easy, try two hands together. Then, try it with eyes closed.

- Coloring activity: orange.

Orange Who?

Knock

knock

Who's

there?

O-   -range

O- -range   who?

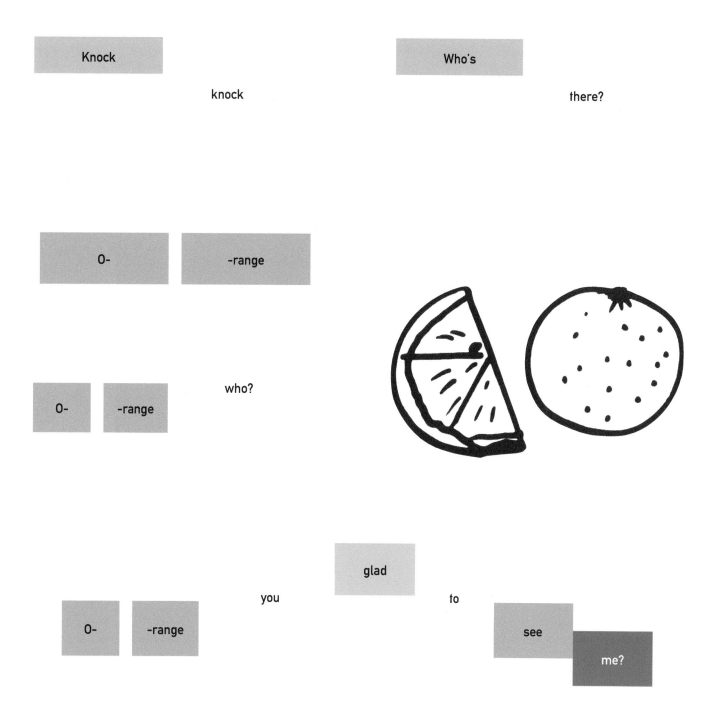

O- -range   you   glad   to   see   me?

1.Introduce

- This song reinforces the patterns learned thus far.

2. Notice & Note

- Ask your child if they notice a pattern.

- Read/sing the words to them while pointing to each box.

3. Demonstrate

- Read/sing the words to them while pointing to each box.

- Sing and play to demonstrate.

4. Now It's Your Turn

- Encourage them to sing and play at the same time. This keeps good rhythm.

- Gently correct the fingering - try to use the right color for the right finger.

5. Practice Notes

- Work on this one hand at a time. When it gets easy, try two hands together. Then, try it with eyes closed.

- Coloring activity: apple.

Red Is For Apples

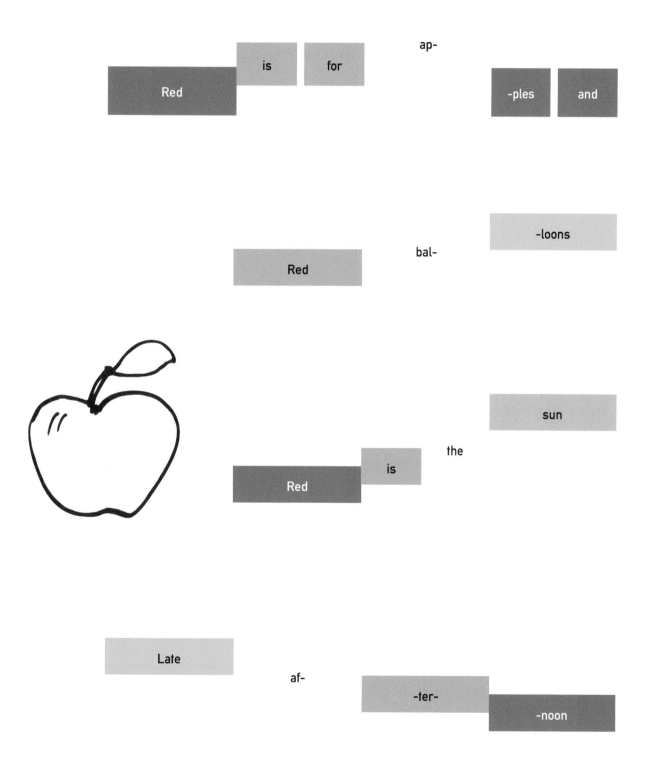

Red is for ap- -ples and

Red bal- -loons

Red is the sun

Late af- -ter- -noon

1.Introduce

- A great song for kids who can't sit still!

- This song is bouncy, fast and fun!

2. Notice & Note

- Ask your child if they notice a pattern.

- Read/sing the words to them while pointing to each box.

- Explain :‖ repeat sign - play it again.

3. Demonstrate

- Read/sing the words to them while pointing to each box.

- Sing and play to demonstrate.

- Use the whole arm when bouncing repeated notes

- It may be more fun to stand while playing.

4. Now It's Your Turn

- Encourage them to sing and play at the same time. This keeps good rhythm.

- Gently correct the fingering - try to use the right color for the right finger.

5. Practice Notes

- Work on this one hand at a time. When it gets easy, try two hands together. Then, try it with eyes closed.

- Coloring activity: ants.

Ants In My Pants

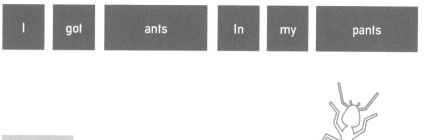

I got ants In my pants

They make me dance!

I got ants In my pants

Yeah Oh

Oh Yeah!

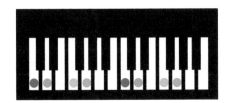

1.Introduce

- Another fast, bouncy song.

2. Notice & Note

- Ask your child if they notice a pattern.

- Read/sing the words to them while pointing to each box.

3. Demonstrate

- Try clapping along while singing it at first.

- Read/sing the words to them while pointing to each box.

- Sing and play to demonstrate.

- Use the whole arm when bouncing repeated notes.

4. Now It's Your Turn

- Encourage them to sing and play at the same time. This keeps good rhythm.

- Gently correct the fingering - try to use the right color for the right finger.

5. Practice Notes

- Work on this one hand at a time. When it gets easy, try two hands together. Then, try it with eyes closed.

- Coloring activity: bongo drums.

Bingo Bongo Boom

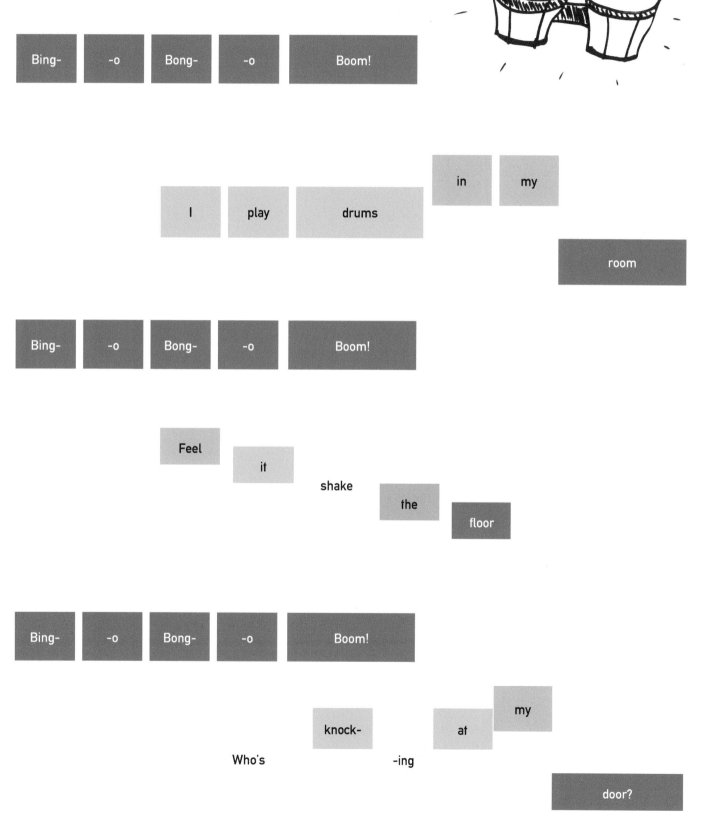

Bing- -o Bong- -o Boom!

I play drums in my room

Bing- -o Bong- -o Boom!

Feel it shake the floor

Bing- -o Bong- -o Boom!

Who's knock- -ing at my door?

1. Introduce

- A funny story song

2. Notice & Note

- Ask your child if they notice a pattern.

- Read/sing the words to them while pointing to each box.

3. Demonstrate

- Try clapping along while singing it at first.

- Read/sing the words to them while pointing to each box.

- Sing and play to demonstrate.

- Use the whole arm when bouncing repeated notes.

4. Now It's Your Turn

- Encourage them to sing and play at the same time. This keeps good rhythm.

- Gently correct the fingering – try to use the right color for the right finger.

5. Practice Notes

- Work on this one hand at a time. When it gets easy, try two hands together. Then, try it with eyes closed.

- Coloring activity: zebra and pizzas.

The Zebra Who Only Ate Pizza

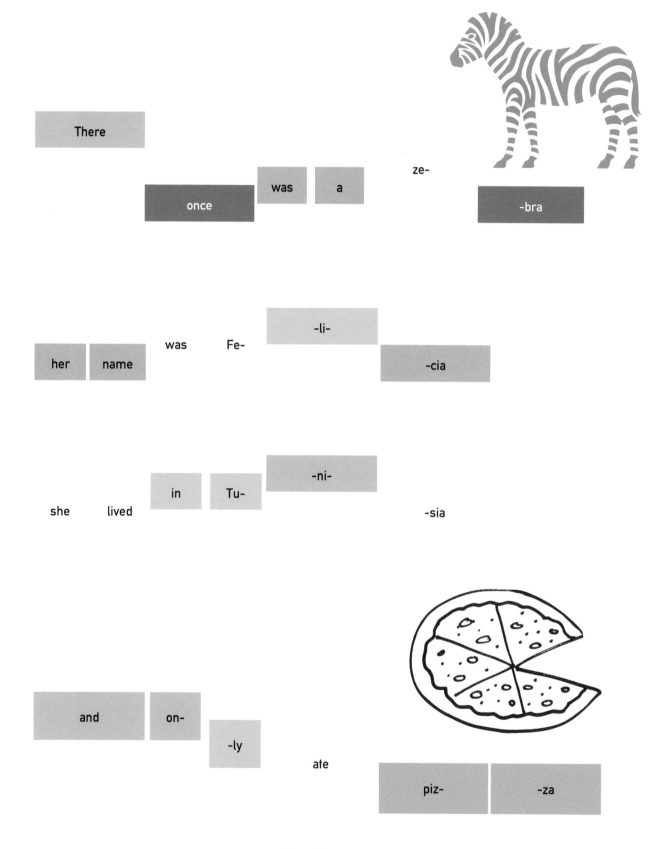

There

once was a

ze-

-bra

her name was Fe- -li- -cia

she lived in Tu- -ni- -sia

and on- -ly ate piz- -za

Zebra 2

What a cra- -zy ze- -bra

on- -ly eats piz- -za

Ev- -'ry- -bod- -y knows

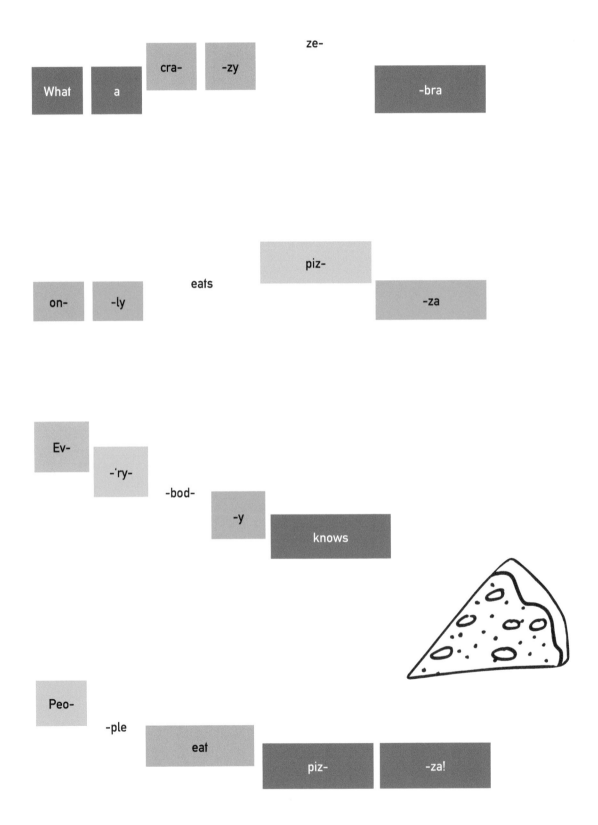

Peo- -ple eat piz- -za!

When your child can sing and play all ten songs from memory with both hands, award them this certificate.

MUSICOLOR METHOD

ACHIEVEMENT
CERTIFICATE

IS HEREBY AWARDED TO

_____

STUDENT NAME

FOR SUCCESSFULLY REACHING

LEVEL 1

_____

DATE

_____

TEACHER

PARENT / TEACHER APPENDIX

SONGS IN STANDARD NOTATION

Song #1 | WHAT'S YOUR FAVORITE ICE CREAM?

WHAT'S YOUR FAV – 'RITE ICE CREAM? WHAT'S YOUR FAV – 'RITE ICE CREAM?

What's your fav-'rite ice cream? What's your fav-'rite ice cream? What's your fav-'rite ice cream? Let's Go have some now!

Song #2 | BIRTHDAY CAKE

BIRTH -DAY CAKE, BIRTH -DAY CAKE, SOME FOR ME AND SOME FOR YOU, BIRTH -DAY CAKE,

Song #3 | LET'S JUMP IN THE POOL

IT'S SO VE-RY HOT OUT-SIDE NINE-TY NINE DE-GREES TO-DAY I DON'T WANT TO STAY IN-SIDE LET'S JUMP IN THE POOL AND PLAY!

Song #4 | DINAH

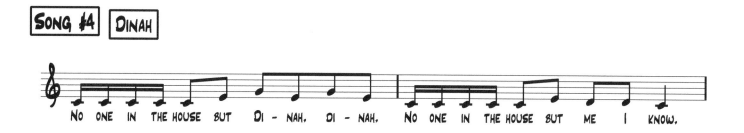

NO ONE IN THE HOUSE BUT DI - NAH, DI - NAH, NO ONE IN THE HOUSE BUT ME I KNOW.

NO ONE IN THE HOUSE BUT DI - NAH, DI - NAH, PLAY - ING ON THE OLD BAN - JO!

SONG #5 | **WHO'S THAT TAPPING?**

WHO'S THAT TAP - PING AT THE WIN - DOW? WHO'S THAT TAP - PING AT THE DOOR?

MOM - MY'S TAP - PING AT THE WIN - DOW, DAD - DY'S TAP - PING AT THE DOOR

SONG #6 | **ORANGE WHO?**

KNOCK KNOCK, WHO'S THERE? O - RANGE. O - RANGE WHO? O - RANGE YOU GLAD TO SEE ME?

SONG #7 | **RED IS FOR APPLES**

RED IS FOR AP - PLES AND RED BAL - LOONS! RED IS THE SUN LATE AF - TER - NOON!

SONG #8 | **ANT'S IN MY PANTS**

I GOT ANTS IN MY PANTS THEY MAKE ME DANCE OH YEAH! OH YEAH!

Song #9 — Bingo Bongo Boom!

BING - O BONG - O BOOM! I PLAY DRUMS IN MY ROOM! BING - O BONG - O BOOM

FEEL IT SHAKE THE FLOOR! BING - O BONG - O BOOM! WHO'S KNOCK - ING AT MY DOOR?

Song #10 — The Zebra Who Only Ate Pizza

THERE... ONCE WAS A ZE - BRA HER NAME WAS FE - LI - CIA SHE LIVED IN TU - NI - SIA AND ON - LY ATE PIZ - ZA.

WHAT A CRA - ZY ZE - BRA ON - LY EATS PIZ - ZA E - V'RY - BO - DY KNOWS PEO - PLE EAT PIZ - ZA!

PRACTICE TIPS

★ FOR MUSIC TEACHERS & PARENTS ★

THE GAME OF
PRACTICE
With 53 Tips to Make Practice Fun!

BY ANDREW INGKAVET
FOUNDER

MUSICOLOR
METHOD

ABOUT PRACTICE

Practice is essential for learning any new skill. In the beginning, it takes willpower. But by creating a routine, you can then turn it into a habit. We are creatures of habit and by consciously choosing which habits to cultivate, we are designing our lives.

HOW MUCH TO PRACTICE

The best option is short sessions daily. In the beginning, five or ten minutes is more than enough. It makes it less overwhelming. You can always practice longer, but try not to miss a day.

WHEN TO PRACTICE

Pick a time of day when you can practice consistently. Perhaps it's before breakfast, before school, or right after school? Before dinner can work too. By scheduling it at the same time everyday, it makes it easier to become a routine. When my son was young, he would practice right before school. As he got older, it shifted to not only after dinner, but also anytime he feels bored. Music has become a constant companion in his life

WHERE TO PRACTICE

Some parents make the mistake of putting the instrument in a far-off corner or playroom. This is almost certain to fail. Children long to be around their parents and family. Being told to go practice in isolation is like telling them to go to the practice dungeon! Put the piano/keyboard in the center of the living area. You will be amazed at how much more they want to play. They may play it multiple times a day, even every time they walk past!

HOW TO PRAISE PRACTICE

Kids need love and attention. They seek your approval. No matter how many times you've heard this piece, you need to praise their effort! The more you take an interest, the more they will be encouraged. But be specific about what you praise. Avoid a general comment like "good job!" Try and find a specific thing or even just focus on effort. By praising specifically, you are actually fostering a growth mindset full of grit. You can learn more about this in Dr. Angela Duckworth's excellent book Grit: The Power of Passion and Perseverance.

WHAT TO PRACTICE

Each lesson presents a single song. These songs are building technique. Don't try to learn too many too soon or out of order. I recommend one song per week, with lots of practice to "get the song in their fingers, minds, and bodies."

Each practice session should be spent working on the current song and any other previous songs. Encourage singing along as it will help them keep a steady rhythm.

MUSICOLOR
METHOD

Practice Chart

WEEK OF	SUN	MON	TUES	WED	THURS	FRI	SAT

Lightning Source UK Ltd.
Milton Keynes UK
UKHW051101150222
398699UK00002B/113